HOW TO DO
SUCCESSFUL
SCIENCE PROJECTS

REVISED EDITION

HOW TO DO
SUCCESSFUL
SCIENCE PROJECTS

NORMAN F. SMITH

REVISED EDITION

JULIAN MESSNER

Copyright © 1982 (How Fast Do Your Oysters Grow? First edition
title), 1990 by Norman F. Smith
All rights reserved including the right of
reproduction in whole or in part in any form.
Published by Julian Messner, a division of
Silver Burdett Press, Inc., Simon & Schuster, Inc. Prentice Hall
Bldg., Englewood Cliffs, NJ 07632. USN&WR graphics copyright©
USN&WR and used with their permission.

JULIAN MESSNER and colophon are trademarks of
Simon & Schuster, Inc.
Design by Malle N. Whitaker.
Manufactured in the United States of America.

Lib. ed. 10 9 8 7 6 5 4 3 2 1
Paper ed. 10 9 8 7 6 5 4 3 2 1

Library of Congress Cataloging-in-Publication Data

Smith, Norman F.
    How to do successful science projects / Norman F. Smith.—Rev.
ed.
        p.   cm.
    Rev. ed. of: How fast do your oysters grow? 1982.
    Includes bibliographical references.
    Summary: Describes how to select a science project, plan the
investigation, choose equipment and test procedures, record data,
draw conclusions, and report the results.
    1. Science projects—Juvenile literature. [1. Science projects.
2. Experiments.]   I. Smith, Norman F.   How fast do your oysters
grow?   II. Title.
Q163.S57   1990
507.8—dc20   90-5456
ISBN 0-671-70685-3   ISBN 0-671-70686-1 (soft)   CIP
                                                                 AC

CONTENTS

To my Grandchildren:

Corbin Michael Smith
Hans Frederick Smith
Rachel Lynn Smith

HOW TO DO
SUCCESSFUL
SCIENCE PROJECTS

REVISED EDITION

INTRODUCTION

The most important work of the scientist is *investigation* and *discovery*. Using observations and measurements, scientists have investigated our natural world to discover its secrets, thereby building the body of scientific knowledge that we have about our universe.

Why is it then that science students rarely choose science projects dealing with investigation and discovery?

The popular projects utilizing model making, collecting, posters, show-and-tell, and laboratory demonstrations may be connected in some ways with science. The student may learn from such projects some of the things that scientists have already discovered. But students will not experience the essence of science, will not learn what scientists really *do*, until they perform an investigative project and make some discoveries for themselves.

A student should experience investigation and discovery whenever possible in science projects. This book will show that simple, interesting, investigative projects are all around us in everyday life, and will describe in detail how one might choose, organize, perform, and report such a project. The emphasis is on simple, single-element projects that can be used as an introduction to investigative science. Such projects are suitable for first-timers because few advanced investigative tools such as controls, statistics, and the like are needed. These tools are therefore mentioned only briefly. The student should seek additional information in more advanced books when he or she is ready for them.

Once a topic has been selected for investigation, success of the project depends entirely upon how well it is planned and executed. Consequently, a large part of this book deals with simplified general procedures for planning the project, performing the investigation, recording and analyzing data, and reporting the results. These procedures are illustrated with examples from the type of simple investigative projects that are the main thrust of the book. These procedures may be applied to science and research investigations at almost any level.

A short list of books covering other aspects of science projects and scientific methods is included at the end of this volume.

CHAPTER I

WHAT IS AN "INVESTIGATIVE SCIENCE PROJECT"?

It is unlikely that anyone could ever become an expert on any topic solely by reading about it or by taking a course. Certainly no one ever became a scientist or an expert in any field of science by this method. Reading about the accomplishments of scientists, listening to lectures, and studying science principles will give you some knowledge of science. But you will not really understand science and its processes until you have actually used its tools and its methods.

One of the best ways to experience scientific methods is through a *science project*. Nearly every student will at some time conduct a science project, perhaps in connection with a *science fair*.

What sort of project should you choose? It is important that the project should be interesting and fun, and should produce results you can be proud of. Most of all, it should help you to experience and learn about the methods of science.

Your first science or science-fair project may be a simple one, such as a poster display about birds, the human heart, or perhaps a demonstration of seed germination or magnets. From such a project you will learn a little about birds, seeds, or magnetism. But you will probably learn only facts that some other scientist has already discovered. You will not be doing what real scientists do: exploring the unknown to discover *new* ideas and *new* knowledge.

To help us understand what science is, we can look at the meaning of the word *science*. Every dictionary defines science in a slightly different way. The *American Heritage Dictionary* says that science is "the observation, identification, description, experimental investigation, and theoretical explanation of natural phenomena." A *phenomenon*, according to the same dictionary, is "an observable event."

In simpler words, in order to experience the methods of science, you must *observe* and *describe* an event that you can see happening, you must *investigate* it with an experiment, and *explain*—or try to explain—what happened. In order to perform a true science project, you cannot merely look up in a book what someone has written about birds, the human heart, or merely plant some seeds. The student scientist must *investigate* something by making measurements, conducting experiments, and making observations to discover something new that he or she did not know before. The discovery need not be earth-shaking or important enough to win the Nobel Prize; it is enough that it is *new to the student*, and is *the product of his or her own investigation*.

Note that it is not necessary to choose an investigation that can be performed in a laboratory setting using test tubes, Bunsen burners, or other laboratory equipment. Nor is it necessary that you investigate a topic that appears in your science book, or in your science course somewhere. Almost *any* topic can qualify as a "natural phenomenon," and can be used as a "science" project. Growing plants, wind, weather, automobile traffic, solar collectors, rocks, fossils, the stock market—all are valid topics with which you can experience and learn about the methods of science. It is especially appropriate that you choose a topic about which you are curious and eager to learn what's happening, why it's happening, what it means, and so on.

The most important reason for studying science in school is to discover how scientists solve problems and investigate the unknown. This will be useful even if you do not eventually work in the field of science. It will help you to organize information, to think about it clearly, and to solve the everyday problems of living in a logical, orderly way.

A second reason for studying science is to learn something about existing scientific knowledge and fundamental science principles so that you can better understand both our physical world and the technological wonders that science has brought us. If you can conduct an experimental investigation, you will also be well equipped to move on to further training as a scientist if you decide to do so.

Before we take up investigative science projects, let's look briefly at all the kinds of projects that are usually done. Through the years, science-fair projects have covered a wide range of topics. This is not surprising, since science is concerned with everything that goes on in our physical world. Yet when we look closely at the projects in a number of science fairs, we find that many of the same projects appear again and again.

Most projects fall into one of about five different categories:

1. Model building (models of the solar system, model volcanoes, clay models of frog organs, etc.)
2. Hobby or pet show-and-tell (arrowheads, dogs, baby chicks, turtles, etc.)

3. Laboratory demonstration (distillation, electrolysis, seed germination, etc., usually right out of the textbook or lab manual)
4. Report with posters (fossils, bees, astronauts, etc., usually from library research)
5. Investigations that produce new information or concrete conclusions (the effectiveness of various detergents, growth rate of oysters, comparison of various insulated containers, survey of seat-belt use, etc.)

The examples listed in the first four categories are not experimental investigations. Although the activities listed under category three are often called science experiments, they are not true experiments but only demonstrations. A true investigation must ask and seek to answer a question. We can convert almost any topic into an investigation *if we ask a question about it.*

For example, a topic about fossils is not in itself an investigative project. But if you ask, "What kind of fossils are found in that layer of rock, and what do they tell us about the age of that rock?" you have a first-rate investigation.

The topic of bees is not an investigative project. Even if you gather all the information you can out of books, you are only reporting what someone else has written. Ask a question like, "Is the rate at which bees make honey greater during some parts of the summer than others?" and you have moved into the realm of science.

Building a solar oven is a construction project, not an investigation. However, if you use the oven to answer the question, "What cooking temperatures can be obtained in full sunlight, partial sunlight, at various times of day?" and so on, you have an excellent investigative project in which you will discover for yourself some new information and some new knowledge.

Projects that ask questions and seek answers through investigations (the fifth category) are true science projects. The student who carries out this kind of project must use the methods of science. You must plan the project yourself, probably do some library research into the recorded facts on your topic, perform an experimental investigation, and analyze your results to obtain some new conclusions or new knowledge. The fact that an investigation like yours may have been performed previously by someone else does not matter. If you plan and set up your *own* investigation, the results you obtain and the conclusions you draw will be truly your own.

If you find that an investigation similar to the one you're planning has been done before, don't panic. See if you can build upon that investigation, and perhaps compare the results of the two—a technique that scientists use whenever they can.

An investigative project may require a little more work, and certainly more thinking, but the results will also be more exciting and much more satisfying. Science projects of this kind are not hard to find. They are all around you in your home, your school, and the world. In the next chapter we will discuss how to choose or "think up" such a project and explore a number of examples.

CHAPTER 2

∧∧∧∧∧∧∧∧∧∧∧∧

CHOOSING A TOPIC FOR YOUR INVESTIGATION

Science students sometimes find it difficult to come up with a topic for a science project. So they try to remember one that they saw at last year's science fair. Or they dig through a science book or lab manual. They're looking in the wrong places. The place to look for science investigations is out in the world. If you look around you like a scientist does, you will see all sorts of things to be curious about. The world is full of things that are taken for granted but have not yet been investigated.

It goes almost without saying that you should choose a project suitable for the terrain and community in which you live. To tackle a project on desert ecology or pond ecology you obviously must have access to these special environments. It may also make sense to choose a topic on which expert advice is available. A project on the stock market, or geology, or solid waste, may be greatly enhanced if you can talk with someone who is enthusiastic about, or deals with, that particular subject. But you should avoid too much involvement of an "advisor," as well as too much dependence upon his or her help. Doing the job yourself, with only the minimum amount of guidance necessary, is the best way.

It's not hard to find an interesting, meaningful project. Let's look at the world around us and find some.

SIMPLE MEASUREMENT PROJECTS

The simplest kind of science investigation is one that makes measurements of something that is already going on. The investigator need not construct the experiment or make any special preparations except to plan the measurements to make and the analysis of the resulting data.

Example 1: Measuring growth of plants. They say that corn grows so fast on a hot summer day in the corn belt of the Midwest that you can *hear* it growing. That's probably a tall story that we needn't waste time investigating, but...how fast does corn really grow? At what size does the corn plant grow fastest? How much can a plant or an ear grow in one day? Do you know?

I don't know, but I would like to find out. If you live on a farm or near one, and if you are interested in a project dealing with growing things, there are plenty of things like this to investigate. To investigate the growth of a corn plant, all you need is a tape measure and a pencil and paper. You will need to think about how many plants you should measure, how often to make the measurements, and how to plot and analyze your data. We'll take up these questions in a later chapter.

We grow zucchini squash in our garden in Vermont every summer. These big green squash grow so fast in hot weather that you have to check them nearly every day to pick them before they get too big. How fast does a zucchini grow? I'd be very interested to find out. A student could very carefully measure the vegetable, or make a tracing of it, or weigh it, or all three, while it is still on the vine. By taking measurements every day, or even several times a day, the rate of growth can be graphed. Some new questions will surely occur to the student-investigator. Does the fruit grow faster on a hot day than on a cool one? How about after a rain or during a dry spell? When the plants are young or old? There is so much to investigate that the student will have to limit the project to only a few things.

If you don't care for squash, there are string beans, tomatoes, cucumbers—take your pick. Again, all you need to do is measure, record, analyze, and graph your data, and you will have some results that every gardener will find interesting.

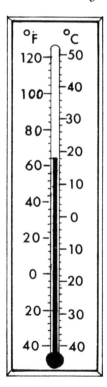

Example 2: The weather. Are you interested in the weather? You are probably familiar with television weather maps showing the cold fronts that move across the country, expecially in the north, at all times of the year. They move swiftly past us, usually bringing a sudden increase in wind, often rain or snow, and always a drop in temperature. How much does the temperature drop as a cold front passes, and how fast? Does the temperature start to move down after the wind strikes or before? How long does the wind blow, and at what speed? Does it shift direction? You can measure outdoor temperatures just by reading the thermometer outside your window. You can measure wind speed and direction with a simple wind gauge, then graph the change in temperature and wind against time and show a "profile" of the cold front. You can visit with a meteorologist in a weather bureau station near you and obtain the barometric variation for that period. If you make your needs known in advance, the meteorologists will probably be able to supply you with a weather map for the front you have measured. Every cold front is different—some are strong, some weak, some wet, some dry—and you need only wait a while for another one to investigate.

Example 3: Tides. If you live on the seacoast, you can measure tides. The normal rise and fall of the tide is not constant; it varies with wind, weather, phases of the moon, etc. If you live in a hurricane area, as I once did, you know that the tide rises very fast and very high as the hurricane approaches. How fast? How high? On a tidal river or creek (*not* on the open coast!), these measurements can be made easily and plotted with wind velocity and time of passage of the hurricane's "eye" to give an interesting picture of the storm.

Example 4: Wind. The wind is being used in some places as a source of energy for generating electricity. With a simple hand-held wind meter than can be bought for five dollars or so, you can measure the wind speed and direction throughout the day. If you live near the seacoast, during some seasons there are offshore winds during part of the day, and onshore winds during the rest. You can measure them and then go into the library to investigate why what you have measured happens. Can you draw some conclusions as to the usefulness of the wind in your area?

Example 5: Temperature of water. Pherhaps you live near a lake or pond. How fast does the water warm up in the spring or cool off in the fall? How much does the temperature change in just one cold (or hot) night? When you're swimming you've probably noticed that the water sometimes seems to be warm on top and shockingly cold toward the bottom. Is that really true? How much is the difference in temperature? You can measure it and find out.

Example 6: Astronomy. For students with an interest in astronomy, there are many projects on the movement of sun and moon, measurement of the angle that the earth's axis and moon's axis make to the ecliptic; and others. Measurements of the rate at which sunrise and sunset points travel across the horizon can be made through the seasons. Photographs of the rising or setting of sun or moon against a distinctive skyline of hills or buildings would provide dramatic illustrations to accompany your measurements. Popular books on astronomy contain information and directions for such experiments.

There are endless possibilities for interesting things about the wind, water, and air, and about the earth's growing things that can be measured with simple intruments, such as a ruler, thermometer, calendar, clock, or camera.

INVESTIGATIONS
YOU CAN PLAN AND CONDUCT

This is the kind of investigation that you can set up to measure how one thing varies with another. For example, how rapidly does a hot liquid cool off in various kinds of insulated containers?

Example 7: Comparison of insulated containers. How do a vacuum (thermos) bottle, a plastic jug, and a plain glass bottle compare in their ability to keep liquids hot?

Is this useful information? If you were going on an all-day fishing trip and wanted to know which container you should use to keep your hot chocolate nice and hot, the results of such an investigation would be very useful.

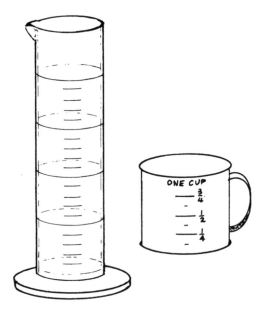

The investigation can be quite simple, using whatever containers you wish and boiling hot water as your test liquid. A thermometer and a clock are used to measure the temperature at various intervals as the liquid cools down.

You need to think the project over carefully and prepare a test plan (Chapter 3) before you start. If the thermos holds a pint and the plastic jug a quart, how do you make the test comparable? Should each container be closed? Will taking the top off of each container to measure the temperature cause inaccurate results? Should the containers be heated before you start? What time intervals should you use? This kind of investigation is a very good one to start with to learn investigative methods. There are, however, so many variables that such an investigation must be very carefully planned to get good results.

Example 8: Performance of cooking pots. How much time or energy, or both, is needed to bring water to a boil in cooking pots made from various materials: cast (heavy) aluminum, stamped (thin) aluminum, cast iron, stainless steel, copper, enameled iron, etc.? The results of such an investigation will tell us which material is the most energy efficient. Care must be taken in choosing the cooking pots to be tested. For example, the pots should be of the same diameter so that the area exposed to the stove burner or element will be the same for each. Some other things to investigate: which uses less electricity—heating water to a boil with the burner on high, medium, or low heat? What if you use a small pot or a large one?

Example 9: Freezing water pipes. I've had radiator pipes freeze and burst in my house twice in recent years. How long does it take a water pipe to freeze when the temperature is, say, 10°F below freezing? How much longer would it take if the pipe were insulated? How many times will a pipe freeze and thaw before bursting? If you live in a cold climate, experiments like these can be performed on a few very cold nights in your garage or on your open porch.

Example 10: Growing plants. There are a number of experiments that can be performed with growing plants: growth in different soils, with different fertilizers, different amounts of sunlight, etc. Measurements can be taken as required to show growth of plant, growth of fruit, or whatever is desired.

Example 11: Human horsepower. How much "horsepower" can a person generate with his muscles? This can be measured by timing a person's climb of a flight of stairs of known height. Is "horsepower" different for people of different age, weight, etc.?

Example 12: Solar collectors. The collection of solar energy can be demonstrated with a homemade insulated box fitted with a tight glass cover and a thermometer inside to measure the temperature. This simple device can also be used to conduct investigations on solar collectors. How does the temperature inside the box (or in a simulated collector tube) change with various conditions such as:

- ▲ angle of the sun to the glass surface
- ▲ color of the inside surface (e.g., black or white)
- ▲ outside air temperature
- ▲ time of day

Does a plastic cover give higher or lower temperatures than a glass cover? Are two pieces of glass better than one?

Example 13: Growth of oysters. If you live near salt water, and if you like oysters, or even if you don't, the growth of oysters would make an interesting project over a year or two. Tiny young oysters called "seed" oysters are easy to obtain (sometimes you can just pick them up on a quiet shore). Suspended in the water beneath a pier on wooden racks or crates, the oysters can be hauled out periodically and weighed, measured, and photographed. By graphing their growth over time, the investigator can learn not only how long they take to grow to market size but also how the growth speeds up and slows down during the year. The investigator might also learn what percentage of the oysters he or she raises die before maturity, how the ratio of meat to shell changes with oyster size, etc. If your oysters have been grown in unpolluted water from which seafood can be eaten, you may enjoy eating the experimental animals after the investigation is over. A little lemon or cocktail sauce will go well with the oysters, raw or cooked (check with your parents or your advisor first).

INVESTIGATIONS BASED UPON CURRENT PROBLEMS

Our civilization faces a host of serious environmental and community problems, such as the "greenhouse effect" or CO_2 problem, the threat to the earth's ozone layer, the solid waste problem, motor-vehicle pollution, and others. Many problems, such as CO_2 and ozone, are too global and too complex to be treated in an investigative science project. But some, such as the solid waste problem, have a direct connection with our own households and our own lives, and may be manageable subjects for science investigations.

Example 14: Solid waste and recycling. Solid waste and garbage are not pleasant topics, but if it's *your* garbage, it isn't so bad to investigate. What does your household waste consist of? How much is food waste, how much plastic, metal, glass, paper, etc.? You could weigh everything on a daily basis for a week or a month and find out. What is the record of, or the prospects for, recycling newspapers, plastics, metal, and glass in your community? Can you plot graphs of change and progress? What about the landfill problem? How does the future look to you, based upon your investigation? Local officials will likely have some data and information on the size of the problem, progress in your community, and other questions to supplement your own observations and analysis.

Example 15: Composting. One solution to the problem of garbage and biomass waste is composting. You can conduct experiments on this technique and produce some compost for the family garden or flower beds in the process. Information on composting is readily available in gardening books or through agricultural agencies. The equipment and materials for composting are easy to make and buy. Experiments on composting different biomass materials, such as garden waste, tree leaves, garbage, and grass clippings, using different methods, would make a good project and a useful product.

Example 16: Junk mail. This topic might be treated as part of the "solid waste" item above, but may be a problem large enough to rate analysis as a separate category. (It is at my house, where an astonishing amount of "solid waste" arrives via my mailbox!) What are the various components of the mail at your house in terms of routine correspondence, magazines, unsolicited advertising, unsolicited catalogs, "box holder" or "occupant" items, and so on? How many pounds of each kind of junk mail? How does this vary over the weeks or months? What happens to it at your house? Is this mail a problem? What could or should be done about it?

FINDING INVESTIGATIONS THROUGH CURIOSITY

There are a million things to be curious about in the world. Some might just give us good practice at being curious. Others may make good science projects. Some will require library research as well as investigation and measurements.

The female perch we catch in Lake Champlain in the spring are heavy with eggs. How many eggs are there in a perch? What do they look like under a microscope? What is their history and their future? I've often wondered.

When apple cider gets sharp and bubbly in my refrigerator, what's happening to it and why, and how fast? You can learn some answers from books, of course, but you can also conduct experiments and measurements on cider for yourself, too.

Every spring the trees in my yard seem to explode into full leaf in only a few days—or maybe a few weeks. How fast *do* tree leaves grow? Prints, tracings, or photographs of the same leaves every day (or twice a day) would show what's happening in slow motion. Do the leaves of some trees grow faster than others? Do they change shape as they develop? What about pine trees?

It seems only a matter of hours after I mow my lawn that new dandelion seedpods are standing there defying me again. How fast does a dandelion seedpod grow? How many individual dandelion seeds are there at the peak of dandelion season on an average lawn? You couldn't actually count them all, of course, but making a good, mathematically sound estimate would be a dandy feature of a dandelion project. I hope that someone will send me an answer to that question someday.

Example 17: The stock market. If you are interested in financial or business matters, a "paper experiment" in stock market investing would make an interesting project. An advisor in your family, or a friend, would be of great help. You can obtain information on the stock market and even some market advice from a local stockbroker or brokerage house. After studying this information, make some choices of what stocks you would like to "buy." Assign a certain amount of "money" to be invested. Keep records of your "purchases" and "sales" and record the market prices of your stocks at regular intervals. Plot their value and the total value of your portfolio over at least six months. Read the financial page of your local newspaper or news magazine. Don't expect miracles. Whether you gain or lose, you'll learn a lot about the stockmarket in such a project, and have an interesting experiement to report.

Example 18: Tree rings: If you live in an area where lumbering is done, or if there are large trees being cut somewhere near you, tree rings may make an interesting project. Growth rings that can be seen on the end of a log or on the stump of a cut tree show the growth of that tree—one ring for each year of its life. They tell us many things: the exact age of the particular tree when it was cut down; when compared with other specimens, the relative rate of growth of various species; the differing amount of growth that occurs from year to year, and other factors.

Tree rings have a unique pattern of small and large growth (narrow and wide rings) over the years that has been used to trace and date logs used in buildings constructed as much as several thousands of years ago. By tracing these growth patterns from log to log over the years, the dates of ancient civilizations have been determined with good accuracy. Can you, by measuring and plotting the width of the rings, find similar growth patterns for several trees? Can you measure average growth rates for several varieties of trees (pine, oak, ash, maple, hop hornbeam, poplar, etc.) and make a bar chart of their growth rates? You may be able to talk the wood cutter or lumberman into sawing some thin slices of logs for you to take home for measurement and analysis and for photographing or displaying. Your library will have books on archaeology that will contain material on the science of tree-ring dating.

Example 19: Roadside geology. Early geologists began their study of the earth's interior by examining cuts made in the earth to build roads, railroads, and canals. There are hundreds of times more rock cuts available today than in their day, chiefly on highways. You can see layering, tilting and bending of layers, fracturing of layers, intrusions (new molten rock that was injected between layers or into cracks across layers), rock types, and even find fossils, if you're lucky. Some study of the literature will help you to identify and understand what you observe. You can take photographs and gather samples for display and for analysis in your report. (On interstate highways, there are prohibitions against pedestrians and stopping, so you may have to be satisfied with quick photographs of cuts rather than close examination on these highways.) What do these cuts show about the geology of your area? What kinds of rocks are there, and what is their age and history? Are there fossils, and if so, what kind and age? Sand pits, quarries, and mine shafts can be interesting areas to examine, too. (**Enter such private properties only with the owner's permission and only in the company of an adult.**)

Example 20: Boiling point of water at various altitudes. People who live at high altitudes find that it takes longer to cook food, because altitude affects the temperature at which water boils. How rapidly does boiling point change with altitude? You can find out if you live in a mountainous area and have a trail on which you can climb a couple of thousand feet. You can make your measurements with only a camping stove or a can of Sterno, a cook pot, some water, a thermometer, and an instrument to measure altitude— either a barometer or an altimeter like those found in a airplane or a car.

At high altitudes, some people use pressure cookers to make possible cooking at higher pressure, with higher temperatures and shorter cooking times. At what altitude does this become necessary or desirable? In this project you could find out.

SURVEY PROJECTS

Surveys make good science projects, and the available topics are almost unlimited. There are many problems before us today having to do with automobile safety, use, and pollution that will make good science projects.

For any of the next four projects, it would be wise to seek the advice of an adult. Do not interfere with traffic in any way, or expose yourself to any danger from vehicles.

Example 21: Automobile seat belts. With efforts to cut highway fatalities and injuries bringing increased emphasis and new laws on wearing seat belts, their use makes a timely project. Seat-belt use can be investigated by sampling students in your school. How many wear a belt regularly? How many families have a firm rule about wearing belts? You can check some of their responses against the general public with a survey out in traffic. Standing near an intersection or a place where cars slow down and seat harnesses can be easily seen, you can make a count for yourself. (You may need mechanical counters that you can hold in each hand to click off your count.)

If traffic is too heavy to check and count every car that passes, you may have to resort to "sampling," a common practice in scientific investigations. In sampling the traffic, you would count every third, or fifth, or tenth car, or whatever you can handle. If you take your sample consistently, you should have a valid sampling of the passing traffic. One special problem: a shoulder harness can generally be seen from outside the car, but many older cars have only seat belts, with no shoulder harness. You must therefore *not* assume that if you don't see a harness, the occupant is not wearing a belt. Could you interpret your highway data better by asking in your student survey how many family cars have belt-and-harness and how many belts only? Sampling and interpreting the results of one survey with another are acceptable, routine processes in science investigations. Attitudes of students in your sample toward seat-belt use would make another interesting phase of your investigation.

Example 22: Traffic-light performance. Somewhere in your town or city there's probably at least one annoying traffic light that drivers grumble about. With a clipboard, counter, and stop watch, you can check it out. Does the light turn red and green on too short a cycle? Does the light stay red too long in one diretion and pile up more traffic from that direction than from the other? Does it change too quicky to stop main-line traffic when activated by a car approaching from a side street? Do you see a significant problem in pollution and waste of fuel caused by vehicles just waiting with their engines idling? Does that traffic light do an equally bad (or equally good) job during rush hours as during the rest of the day? If you find that the light is really not doing its job well, it could be in need of adjustment. Send a copy of your report to the Mayor or the Chief of Police— they should be interested.

Example 23: Vehicle speed in a speed zone. There's probably also a place in your town or on your highway where some vehicles appear to be exceeding the speed limit. A check on this requires some careful planning and perhaps more than one observer. Perhaps you could team up with one or two other young scientists for this project. To measure vehicle speed, you need an accurately measured distance and a very accurate measurement of the time required for vehicles to travel that distance.

Carefully measure with a steel tape the distance between two telephone poles or other markers several hundred feet apart. Measure the time for each vehicle in your sample to travel this distance. (If you cannot accurately measure the time of passage from one location, start your stopwatch at the first marker and have your assistant at the second marker signal the instant of passage by a hand signal or other means, such as a walkie-talkie.) Record each measurement for later calculation of vehicle speed.

Try to get a regular sample, that is, every fifth or tenth vehicle, or whatever you select as appropriate. Do *not* be influenced in your choice of vehicles to time by the kind of car, by its speed, or any other factor—stick to your sampling interval rigorously and ignore all other vehicles. Some hints on the plotting of data from such a project will be found in Chapter 6.

Example 24: Number of occupants in commuter vehicles. Carpooling can yield substantial reductions in vehicle use, and thereby have a large effect on fuel conservation and vehicle pollution. How many commuter vehicles carry only one person; how many carry two, three, four, or more? You can find out with a simple survey taken at the entrance to a municipal parking lot or garage at any hour, or at a company parking lot at employee arrival times. How many students carpool, or walk, or ride bikes, or take the bus to school? Are these numbers changing from year to year? A survey of students or a count at the school parking lot could be made to obtain this sort of information.

LIBRARY-RESEARCH PROJECTS

Library-research projects may or may not be investigative projects. A project on the general topic of fossils, for example, will reveal only facts that other scientists have already discovered. Such a project will bring to the student some scientific knowledge of fossils, but it will be more of an essay project than a scientific investigation. It will not give the student experience in performing a scientific investigation.

On the other hand, look at the photograph of a fossil shown in Figure 2-1. This fossil was found on a large boulder on a beach on Lake Champlain. The following questions could help you begin your research:

FIGURE 2-1. **This is a fossil that was found on a boulder near Lake Champlain.**

▲ What sort of creature is it?

▲ When did it live?

▲ What was the world like in those days?

▲ What is the geological history of this area?

▲ How were the creature's remains (or imprint) preserved?

▲ How is this creature related to creatures alive on earth today?

These (and other) questions constitute a real investigative project. In such a project you would not just be looking up scientific information, you would also be using this information to investigate this fossil, to answer a particular question, or to learn something new about the world beneath your feet.

By pursuing such an investigation you will learn another important fact: you are not likely to find exact, complete answers to all of the preceding questions. The scientific information that now exists on fossils was compiled from studying just such evidence as the fossil in Figure 2-1, and is probably still being added to and improved. It is possible that a new fossil may bring new questions that cannot be answered now, or may even disprove some things that scientists had believed before.

Subjects like this one are all around us. Another topic for an investigative project is shown in Figure 2-2. These curious samples of rocks were gathered on another Lake Champlain beach.

▲ How did the layer of hard, white rock become sandwiched between two layers of softer, gray rock in the large sample at left?

▲ What kinds of rocks are these?

▲ What is the geology of these rocks and how were they made?

▲ How old are they?

▲ Are their ages the same?

▲ How did the rocks at right develop large holes all the way through them?

FIGURE 2-2. These rocks were gathered near Lake Champlain.

Can these questions be answered by using the science of geology? It is possible. In such a project, it will be up to the student to search out the scientific information that is available and apply it to the item being investigated. In doing so, the student will be discovering something that he or she did not know before.

When you get an idea for a project, write it down quickly, before you forget it. Then you can think about it and begin to plan your investigation. The examples in this chapter will probably give you ideas for other projects that will fit your interests and your own experiences. There will be more ideas for projects scattered through the rest of this book. Watch for them.

CHAPTER 3

PLANNING YOUR
INVESTIGATION

As the old saying has it, "Anything that is worth doing is worth doing well." It follows that doing anything well is almost sure to require extra time and effort.

Investigative science projects are no exception. If you choose such a project because you believe that it will be worth doing, you will want to do it well and will likely need more time and perhaps a little more effort to do so.

Some of this effort should go into *planning* the project. Any investigation is made up of a number of steps that must be organized. Careful planning is needed if these steps are to be performed in an orderly fashion and are to yield good results. Failure to plan the project in advance can cause a waste of time and effort, and may lead to poor results or even failure of the project.

Proper planning should include a carefully prepared plan of action, or *test plan,* written down in as much detail as possible.

A student we'll call Jerry once started a science project with only the vague idea that he was going to investigate how hot certain materials, such as wood, cloth, paper, crayons, etc., had to be before they would catch fire. Jerry didn't think his project through or prepare a test plan. In trying to get his equipment together, he found that he could not obtain the instruments needed to measure "kindling" temperatures, as they are called, but he did locate a stopwatch. He decided to change his project to investigating *how long* it took these materials to catch fire after being placed in a pan heated from below by a bunsen burner. Jerry still didn't prepare a test plan, but he did keep a log of everything he did. The log showed that some things caught fire quickly while some took longer. But some didn't catch fire at all; instead, they merely charred, shriveled up, melted, or smoked. After a number of experiments, Jerry realized that he could not make useful comparisons and therefore could not draw any conclusions from his investigation.

Jerry's problem was that he had not made sure before starting that he had a plan of action and test methods that were likely to yield useful, meaningful results. If he had done so, he might have wondered whether his procedures would work, and perhaps would have made a few quick test runs to check them out. He would have discovered early that he was not likely to get useful results. He would have then needed to rethink his whole project idea and either change it greatly or abandon it for a new one. Although the scientist (and the science student) still learns something from an unsuccessful investigation, a successful project is far more productive and satisfying.

THE TEST PLAN

The main items to be covered in any test plan are a statement of the purpose of the investigation, descriptions of the equipment to be used and the tests to be conducted, and some idea as to how the data will be gathered and used. These main items will be covered briefly here; some of them will be treated in more detail in following chapters.

Think of your test plan as a flexible document. No one should expect to sit down and write a complete test plan in final finished form the first time. You may find that you can't get the equipment you need to accomplish the project (this will be discussed in the next chapter); you may then need to change the purpose of your investigation. Perhaps a test procedure can't be worked out with the equipment you have, and one or the other must be changed. Or when you think about what you will do with your data, you will find that you will need some other measurements. You may need to go back and rework all the other steps of the test plan in order to come up with a workable project that will yield useful results. If the boy who wanted to measure kindling temperatures had thought through his project to the anaylsis of data, he would have discovered that he had to change the goal of his project, use other methods, or abandon the project for one that could be accomplished.

41

Writing the test plan gives you time to think about your investigation, to test it in your mind to see if it can be done, and to see if it will yield useful results. If you cannot decide upon the steps you should follow and cannot put the test on paper, you may not have a workable project. If you do have a workable project but do not plan the test procedure carefully, you may miss something important and might even have to go back and do some of your work over again to get better results.

Planning your investigation will also help you to schedule the time required to accomplish it. I've heard it said that "the best time to start thinking about next year's science project is the day you finish *this* year's project!" For some investigations, planning far ahead is a must. If you plan to investigate growing plants, your data must be gathered during the summer. If your project concerns snow and ice, it must be scheduled for winter months. If your investigation will be performed in the laboratory or in your kitchen, it can perhaps be done at any time. But an adequate length of time for the various steps of your project must be planned in advance.

The test plan can't possibly solve all your problems, and there will certainly be surprises, errors, and disappointments along the way. After all, you are exploring the unknown in your investigation, and you cannot know in advance what your results will be or what problems you will encounter. But a good test plan lets you think the project through in advance and perform your investigation in an orderly fashion, with enough time and with minimum work, to achieve the best results.

Statement of Purpose You should be able to state briefly the purpose of your investigation. No details are needed, only a general statement of what will be investigated and what you hope to learn. Think your project through as carefully as you can at this stage. You are not committing yourself forever by what you write; you can change it along the way. But the task of setting your idea down on paper will help you to clarify your thoughts and test their suitability for an investigation.

Example: The purpose of this invesigation is to measure the length of time that various kinds of cups will keep liquids hot. Several different kinds of cups will be tested: plastic, pottery, Styrofoam, glass, metal, etc.

Equipment To Be Used You should list all the equipment that you will need to perform the investigation. Keep the list open so that you can add things you forget or discover later.

Example:
>   Stove or burner for heating water
>   Kettle or pan for heating water
>   Thermometer (range __° to __°)
>   Test cups (list them)
>   Clock or watch with second hand
>   Forms and pencil to record data
>   Measuring cup for measuring water

Test Procedure In this section you should state, step by step, the process you will use to perform the investigation.

Example:
1. Draw up a table (form) on paper on which to record the data. Mark it clearly to show what is being tested, etc.
2. Set up cup and thermometer in the work area.
3. Heat measured quantity of water to boiling.
4. Pour boiling water into cup.

5. As soon as temperature reading on thermometer steadies, read temperature and time.
6. At intervals of one minute, read and record temperature. (Intervals can be increased to 2, 5, or 10 minutes, or whatever gives a good curve of change).
7. Repeat investigation in exactly the same way for each kind of cup.

Analysis of Data Although you may no be able to think through every detail, you should describe a general plan as to what you will do with your data: how you will calculate, graph, and analyze it.

Example: Graphs of temperature against time will be made similar to the one in Figure 3-1. These curves should show the different rates of cooling for the different kinds of cups. Perhaps there will be different shapes to the curves. I hope that the curves will show

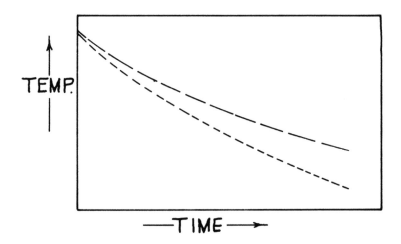

FIGURE 3-1. **Graph of temperature against time.**

which kind of cup you should put coffee into if you want to keep it hot a long time, and which kind you should put it in if you are in a hurry to get your coffee cool enough to drink.

THE REPORT

It would be appropriate to jot down a few notes about how you expect to report and/or display your project and your results. You can then plan for these items as you conduct your project and analyze your results.

JUNE						
s	m	t	w	t	f	s
	1	2	3	4	5	6
7	8	9	10	11	12	13
14	15	16	17	18	19	20
21	22	23	24	25	26	27
28	29	30				

CHAPTER 4

CHOOSING YOUR EQUIPMENT & TEST PROCEDURES

If you worked in a multimillion dollar research laboratory, you might not have to worry about being able to get the equipment you need. But if you are a science student, chances are that getting equipment for your science project may be a problem. Lack of equipment may keep you from doing some things you would like to do, but if you design your investigation carefully to fit the equipment you can find at home or at school, or make for yourself, you can probably do the kind of project you want.

Fortunately, there are many investigative projects that require measurement of only simple variables. A variable may be defined as any quantity that changes or can cause another quantity to change. Examples of simple variables are temperature, time, distance, size, speed, etc. The instruments needed to measure such simple variables are readily available.

Instruments needed to measure more exotic variables, such as electrical voltage, electrical current, electrical power, high temperatures, water flow, pressures, etc., are more difficult to obtain, but some might be found in a good school laboratory. The point is that

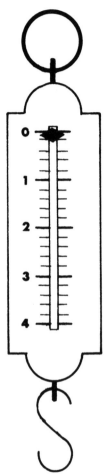

you should choose and design your project to fit not only your own interests and capabilities but also the measurements that you will be able to make. Perhaps talking with your teacher or advisor would help you choose a realistic, feasible topic for your investigation.

In any event, try to avoid investigations that will require fancy, expensive equipment or a large amount of construction. The simpler the equipment required, the better you can concentrate on the investigation itself. For what you do need, use your imagination and try to make creative use of available resources. Remember that what you *discover* in your investigation is the important thing—not the assembly of a huge, impressive array of gadgetry.

Safety should be given full attention while the project is being planned. If the investigation is to be a laboratory project, established rules and procedures should be followed and all safety and protection equipment used. If any hazardous procedures or materials (including fire, boiling water, electricity, chemicals, etc.) are to be used, review the whole project with your teacher or another adult before proceeding. Always use great care and plenty of common sense.

In making measurements of any variables, it is necessary to make certain that the process of measuring does not spoil the experiment. For example, in measuring the temperature changes of liquid in insulated jugs, taking out the cork and inserting a thermometer will allow heat to escape, which will affect the results. If a snug hole is drilled in the cork and a thermometer is inserted through this opening and left in place, this problem will be eliminated. For another example, experiments conducted inside a refrigerator or freezer would be seriously affected by opening the door to take measurements. Measurement of temperatures might be accomplished by means of a thermocouple which requires only a pair of thin wires to transmit the temperature signal to the measuring instrument. The refrigerator door can be closed on the wires without harming them or the measurement. Another remote measuring device that might be used is an indoor-outdoor thermometer, which requires only a thin tube. The temperature-sensing devices could be installed inside the refrigerator, and the readings made from the instrument outside, thus making it unnecessary to open the door.

In planning your detailed test procedures, careful consideration must be given to the variables you will measure. You should think through the range of each variable. How many degrees of temperature? What starting and ending temperatures? How many inches or feet? How long a time? What sort of intervals will be used? For example, how much time should elapse between measurements? For measurements of the change in temperature of heated liquid in a thermos bottle, the measurements might be made once per hour; for measurements of the growth of a plant, once a day, once a week, or whatever seems appropriate. Think these things through and write down a plan of action. If your investigation must be performed at a special time or season, write that down. A project on corn growth must obviously be done in the summer and an investigation of ice thickness on a lake in the winter.

If your project is to measure the growth rate of pumpkins, you should consider such questions as these:

- ▲ How often shall I measure the pumpkin?
- ▲ What shall I measure: weight? diameter? girth?
- ▲ What instruments shall I use for these measurements?
- ▲ How many pumpkins shall I measure?
- ▲ Shall I record or investigate other variables, such as daily temperature, rainfall, how many pumpkins are on the vine, etc.?

While measuring the variable of primary interest, the scientist must always be aware of other variables that may affect the measurements and should seek to eliminate those variables that can be eliminated, measure their effects if these seems important, or at least record these items in case some further investigation is needed.

For example, in a project to measure the growth of corn plants through a growing season, the main variable is *time*. But we can guess that amounts of rainfall and sunshine will have effects. Measurements next summer may not agree with those made last summer because these conditions may be different. Also, the variety of corn planted, the kind of soil in the garden, and the amount of fertilizer used will affect the results.

If it is our goal in a simple investigative project to measure and report the growth of *these* corn plants *this* summer in *this* particular soil, we need not worry about isolating all the variables. But it would be a good practice to record all that we can about other variables— the corn variety planted, the rainfall and sunshine during the period, the type of soil and amount of fertilizer used, etc.—just in case someone wants to compare other results with ours.

On the other hand, if it is the goal of our project to measure the effect of various amounts of fertilizer on the growth of corn plants, the project becomes more complicated. We need to think about *controls*; that is, using some of our experiments to provide a basis for comparison to the rest. For example, in a project on fertilizer, the control plants might be a group that is given *no* fertilizer. Comparison of their growth to the growth of the fertilized plants would give data on the effect of the fertilizer.

But again we have to watch the other variables. Soil might have an effect on the results as might the amount of water fed to the plants. If the plants are in greenhouse pots, we can use the same soil and feed each plant the same amount of water. If all plants are planted in the same garden and exposed to the same rainfall, these variables may also be unimportant. But under some conditions there might be other variables that will affect the experiment. The amount of moisture in the soil probably affects the use of fertilizer by the plant. Experiments performed in the same garden in a wet year may not give the same results as those performed in a dry year. One might ask, also, whether different *types* of soil may not affect the use of fertilizer by the plant.

From this simple example, you can see that the task of totally eliminating unwanted variables, in order to study just one, is extremely difficult, perhaps impossible. All the scientist can do is be alert to the problem and work endlessly to isolate, evaluate, or reduce the effects of variables other than the one(s) he or she wants to study.

FIGURE 4-1. **This graph charts the growth of three groups of corn plants. (Note: data are fictitious)**

The simple investigative projects suggested in this book generally have one main variable that can be readily measured. But as a budding scientist, you should be aware that numerous other variables are lurking in the background. As part of your test planning, you should think about other variables that might affect your results, allow for them in your test procedures, and carefully record, along with your test data, the conditions of these variables in case this information is ever needed.

More complex experiments that require controls may also require more complex methods of analysis of data. For example, suppose that your data on the size of three groups of corn plants looks like the graph in Figure 4-1. The fertilizers seem to have an effect on the growth of the plants in that most of the plants are a little taller than the control group. But which has produced more growth, fertilizer A or B? In many cases it is not possible to tell at a glance, or sometimes even by careful examination, just which results are greater and by how much. In such cases, mathematical and statistical methods can be used to find out whether significant differences have occurred.

These methods are beyond the scope of this book. Science students who need to consider or use these tools of science may find the help they need from their teachers and from books published on the subject, some of which appear in the bibliography shown at the end of this book.

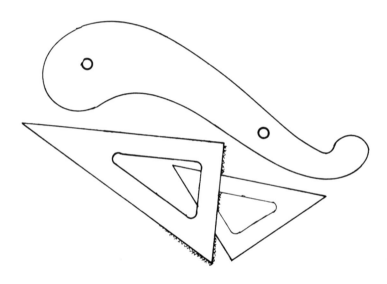

CHAPTER 5

∧∧∧∧∧∧∧∧∧∧∧∧∧∧

RECORDING YOUR DATA

The data you gather in your project are very valuable. These numbers and notes are the product of your hard work. They contain whatever it may be that you have measured and discovered in your project.

It is surprising how many students will try to record their data on a crumpled, dirty scrap of paper or on the back of an old envelope. Something that looks like a scrap of paper will likely be treated as such and thrown away. There goes all your hard work.

It's surprising, too, how fast your memory of what you did in each of your experiments will fade. If you trust your valuable project to the vagaries of memory, you will probably lose some important things. It pays to make a careful record of your experiments on businesslike forms that will leave nothing to memory or to chance.

After you have thought about your test procedures (the topics of Chapters 3 and 4) and drawn up a test plan, you can then prepare for recording your data. A simple test data form is shown in Figure 5-1. The form contains space at the top for the name of the project, the test number, what will be tested and why, and other information,

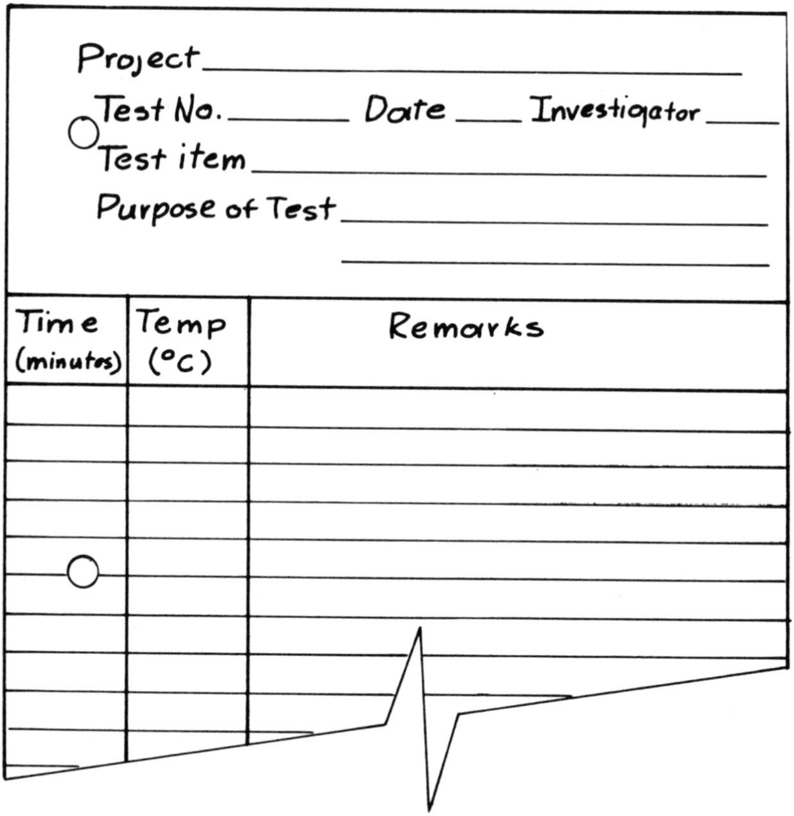

Project_____

Test No._____ Date _____Investigator_____

Test item_____

Purpose of Test_____

_____

Time (minutes)	Temp (°C)	Remarks

FIGURE 5-1. Typical test data form.

along with columns for the measurements. Your form will not be just like this sample, of course, but it will have spaces and columns for the information and the variables that *your* test will consider. A space for remarks is advisable so that you can record anything that you may notice during the test, any happening that might affect the data, or even a sudden idea for another test that you might want to jot down as you think of it.

You can make up a form with a ruler and pen and hand lettering, or type it on a typewriter and make copies on a copying machine if one is available. Or you can type it on a word processor and print as many copies as you need.

Try the form in your first few tests. If it doesn't work well, or if it doesn't have spaces for information you need, change the form as needed.

Be sure to note all conditions of the test so that you will have a record of exactly what you did, what sample you tested, what your purpose was, and so on. Don't be bashful about jotting down anything that happens (or *doesn't* happen!) in the "Remarks" column: "This measurement does not look right," or "My instrument did not work well for this measurement," or "The setup leaked a little here." Such notes may save you a lot of grief later when you're trying to check something or find out why a data point looks strange or incorrect.

For some investigations that involve counting rather than measuring, other types of data forms will be needed. For example, suppose the investigation was a fuel-conservation project aimed at finding out how many people were riding alone and how many were sharing the ride by carrying other passengers. (Such a project is described in Example 24.) Each vehicle in your sample can be recorded as observed by making a check mark or a symbol in the appropriate column of the data sheet shown in Figure 5-2. A "scatter plot" made directly from this data sheet can be used to show such data in the final report, as will be discussed in Chapter 6.

If you will be performing more than just a few tests, you should probably make a test log, too, like that shown in Figure 5-3. This log will give you a handy record of your tests and a quick and easy way to find any test you want to examine.

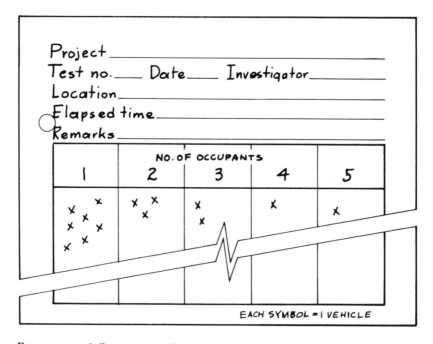

FIGURE 5-2. A "scatter plot" is used as a form for recording test data.

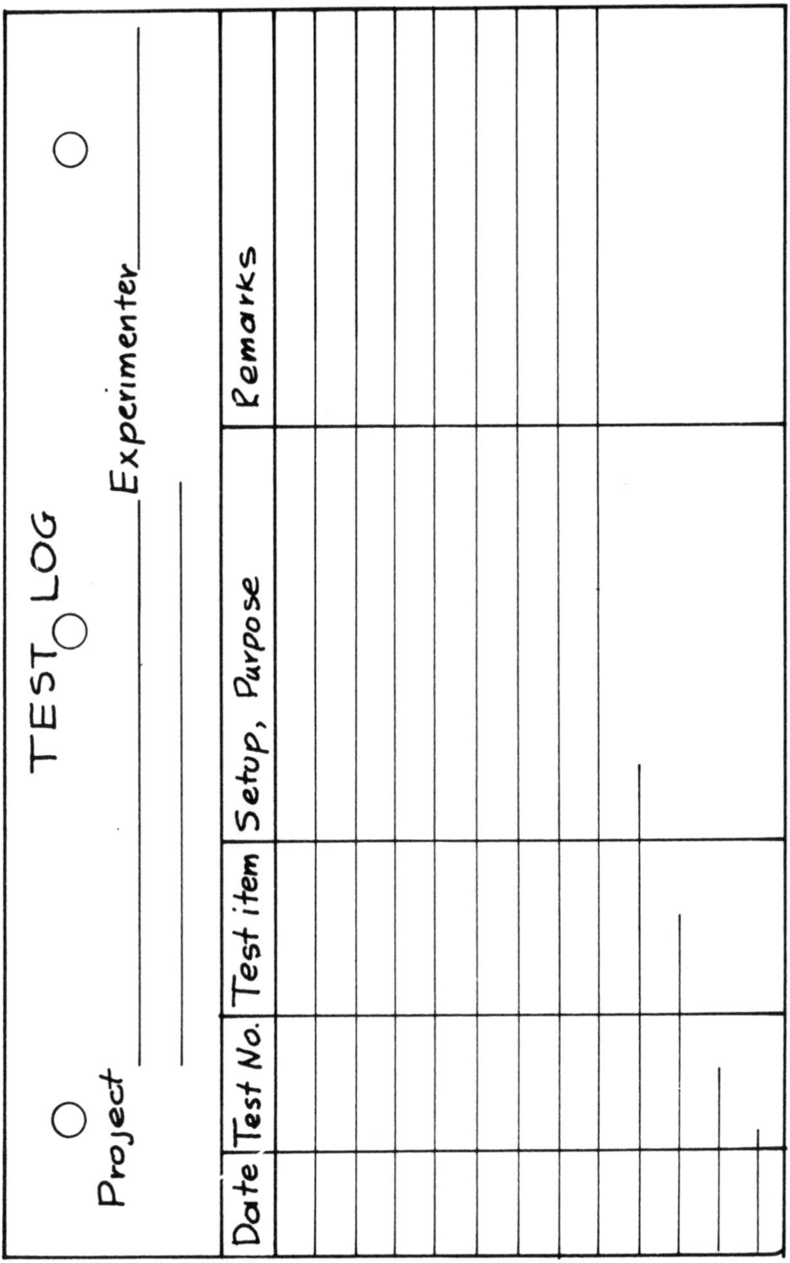

FIGURE 5-3. Typical test log.

Punch holes in the test forms and log sheets and keep them safe and orderly in a ring-bound notebook. During your tests, record your investigations neatly and completely. It's okay to copy a sheet over if it gets messed up during the activity of an experiment. A well-kept notebook containing your data forms and test log is something that you can show proudly as an example of your growing skill as a scientist-experimenter.

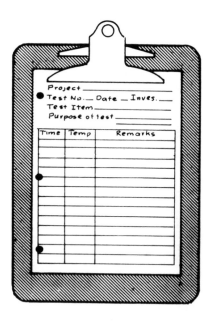

CHAPTER 6

GRAPHING YOUR DATA

When you examine carefully the numbers tabulated on your data forms, you can usually get some idea of what the data shows. You may be able to see, for example, that the temperature you measured decreased with time. But how fast did it decrease? Did it decrease at a steady rate?

The best way to see clearly how one quantity changes with respect to another is to *graph* the data, which can be done in many ways. Graphing your data (and analyzing the graphs) can be one of the most interesting and challenging parts of your experimental project. Good graphs also help you to explain your findings to others.

BASICS OF GRAPHING

Figure 6-1 is a simple graph that shows a change of one variable with respect to another; in this case, a decrease of temperature over

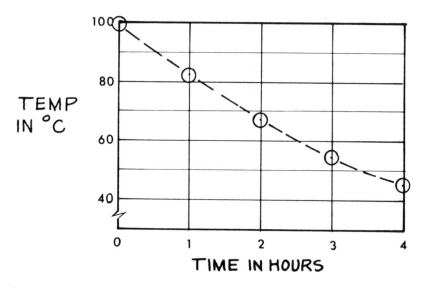

FIGURE 6-1. This is a simple graph of temperature change with time.

time. The circular symbols are drawn to show the *test points*, that is, the temperatures measured and recorded at 1, 2, 3, and 4 hours from the test beginning.

To make such a graph, you will need a piece of graph paper. You can buy graph paper at stationery stores (see photo) or you can make it yourself, as shown in Figure 6-2A.

Place numbers on the vertical and horizontal scales that will cover the ranges of the two variables you measured. Usually the horizontal scale represents the variable that you select for your experiment, the variable that just happens—for example, *time*. This variable is called the *independent variable*.

The vertical scale is usually made the *dependent* variable, or whatever it is that you're measuring against the independent variable—for example, *temperature*.

You may draw as many lines in the grid of your graph as you need to plot your data easily and accurately (Figure 6-2). Note that for this type of graph the numbers on the scales identify the line, not the spaces between lines. Be sure to locate each number exactly opposite the line it labels (Figure 6-1). Place numbers on only as many of these grid lines as you need to make plotting or reading the graph easy.

FIGURE 6-2A. **Many kinds of graph paper can be bought at stationery stores.**

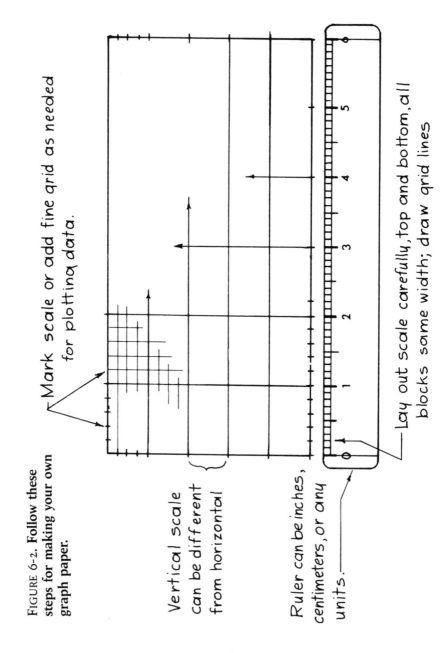

FIGURE 6-2. Follow these steps for making your own graph paper.

Mark scale or add fine grid as needed for plotting data.

Vertical scale can be different from horizontal

Ruler can be inches, centimeters, or any units.

Lay out scale carefully, top and bottom, all blocks same width; draw grid lines

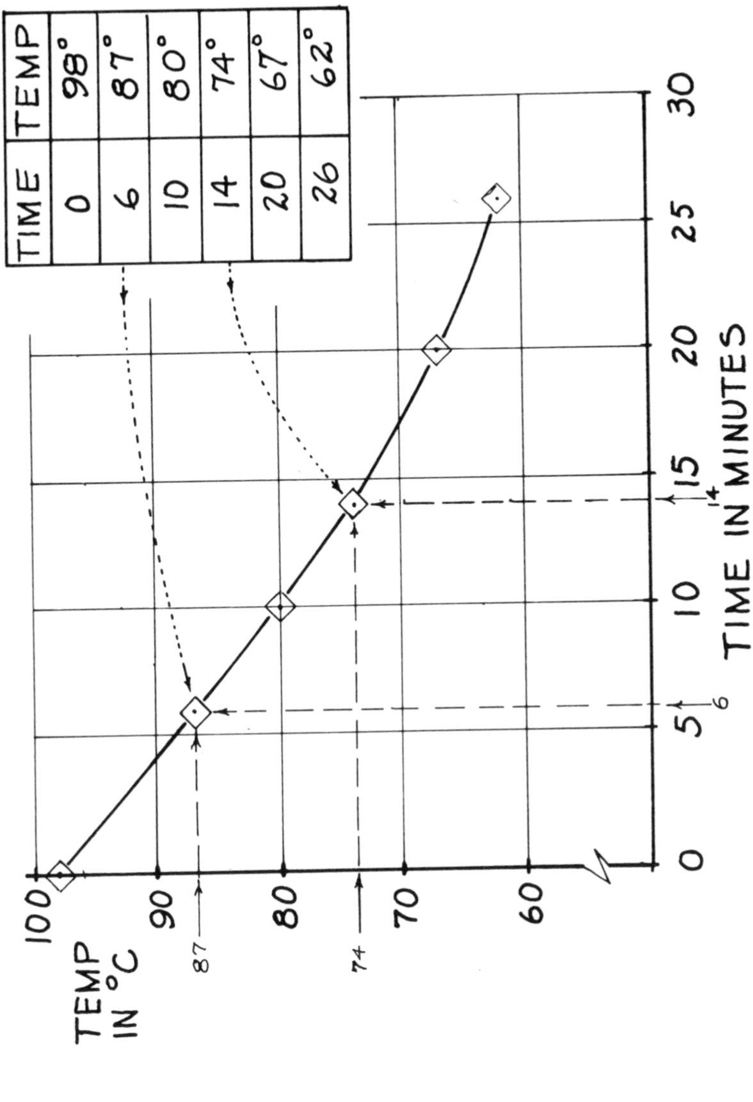

Tabulated data

TIME	TEMP
0	98°
6	87°
10	80°
14	74°
20	67°
26	62°

FIGURE 6-3. This is the technique for plotting a graph.

The procedure for plotting tabulated values on a graph is shown in Figure 6-3. For each data point, enter the bottom of the graph at the value of time (for example, six minutes) and proceed vertically upward until the value of temperature for that time is reached (for example, 87°). Mark this point with the symbol that you have chosen for this particular curve. Plot the other points from your tabulated data in the same way. Connect the data points with a line or curve, and you have a pictorial representation of the variation of temperature over time.

SYMBOLS AND LINE CODES

You may choose your symbols and curves from the typical symbols and line codes shown in Figure 6-4, or make up some original ones if you wish. The curves on your graphs should always

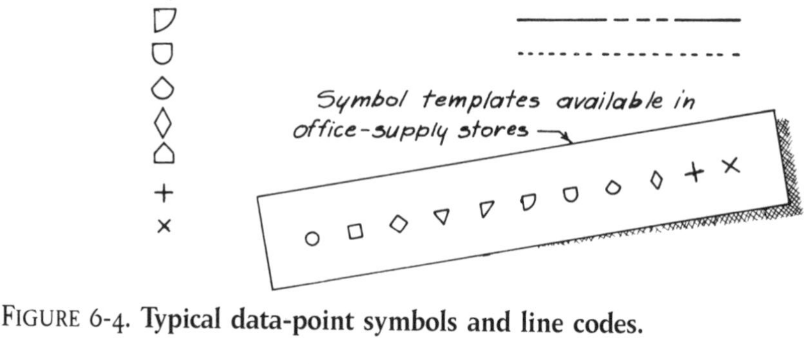

FIGURE 6-4. Typical data-point symbols and line codes.

be clearly labeled. Four ways of labeling are shown in Figure 6-5. Placing labels directly on the curves, as shown in the two upper examples, is often the best way. Where this method is not possible, a table of symbols or lines (or both), as shown in the boxes at the bottom, may be used. Choose the method—or combination of methods—that does the job for your particular graph.

Comparing the results of several tests becomes easier when the data are plotted in graphs. For example, if you were to investigate how well three containers kept a liquid cold, your results in tabulated

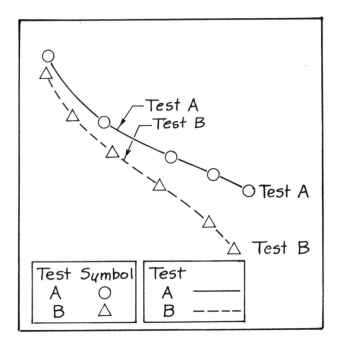

FIGURE 6-5. Here are four ways of labeling curves. Investigators should choose the one that identifies curves clearly and quickly.

FIGURE 6-6. Test data are difficult to compare in tables (left), but easy to compare in a graph (right).

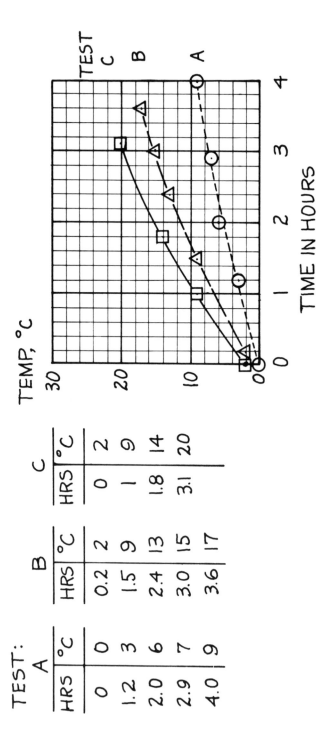

TEST:

A	
HRS	°C
0	0
1.2	3
2.0	6
2.9	7
4.0	9

B	
HRS	°C
0.2	2
1.5	9
2.4	13
3.0	15
3.6	17

C	
HRS	°C
0	2
1	9
1.8	14
3.1	20

form might look like the data shown in the left half of Figure 6-6. (Don't forget as you read this book that all test data shown were made up for illustration only.) You can see just by glancing at the tabulated data that the temperatures for all three tests increase as time passes. A detailed comparison of the three different tests, however, is not easy to make from the table.

When the data are plotted, as in the right half of Figure 6-6, the three tests can be instantly compared. You can tell at a glance that the container used in test A kept the liquid cold much better than either of the other two, and that the container used in test C gave the poorest performance because it allowed the liquid to warm up much faster. With this clear view of what you have measured, you could proceed to explore why these things happened, to draw some

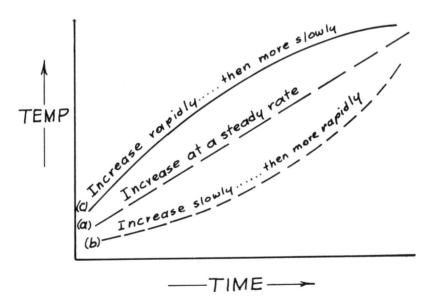

FIGURE 6-7. These three curve shapes indicate different rates of change.

conclusions from your tests, and so on. Note that the time intervals for measuring data are different for each curve, but the curves can nevertheless be compared directly with each other.

There are other things that can be learned from such graphs, depending upon what you are investigating. For example, all sorts of curve shapes can occur. Run your eye (or your finger) along curve (a) in Figure 6-7, and you will see that it indicates a steady (straight-line) increase of temperature with time. Curve (b) shows a condition in which the temperature increases slowly at first, then faster as time goes on. Curve (c) shows a condition in which the temperature increases rapidly at first, then more slowly as time goes on.

Figure 6-8 shows other kinds of curve shapes. See if you can describe how "y" varies with "x" in each case.

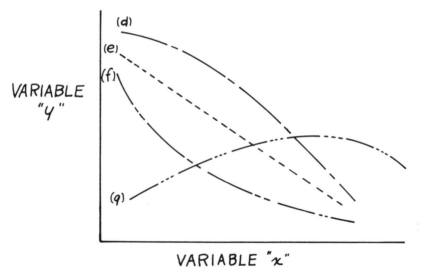

FIGURE 6-8. **Can you describe the changes shown by these curve shapes?**

OTHER KINDS OF GRAPHS

There are many other ways to graph data besides a simple plot of one variable against another. Several other kinds of graphs will be described. It is up to you to choose the method best suited to your project, or invent a new one if you need it.

Suppose your project is to measure the speed of cars and trucks along a stretch of highway to learn how many vehicles are traveling below and above the speed limit. You could do this (as described in example 23) by measuring the time each vehicle takes to travel the measured distance. For each vehicle you can then calculate its highway speed in miles per hour or kilometers per hour.

Your data for a specified amont of time, say one hour, could be tabulated as shown in the left half of Figure 6-9 and plotted on a graph like the one discussed earlier, as shown in the right half of the figure. Such a plot shows at a glance which speed is most common and how many vehicles are exceeding the speed limit.

This graph illustrates why individual data points are generally shown when data is plotted. How will the dependent variable change between data points? Nobody really knows. The graph can be left with no curve between data points. Or for clarity (especially if several sets of data have been plotted), data points can be connected with a smooth, curved line if the scientist thinks the variation between points might be smooth and gradual, or with a series of straight lines if appropriate. In any event, the reader will know from the data points that measurements were made only at those points. The reader will use his or her own judgment if the graph is to be read between data points.

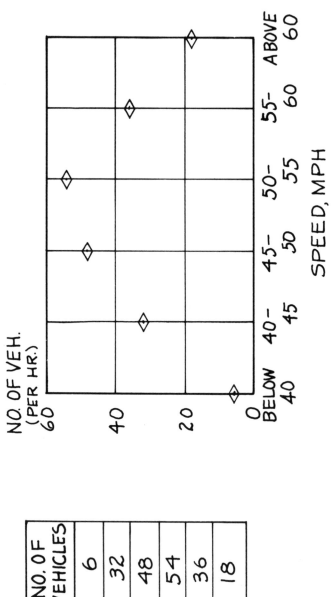

FIGURE 6-9. Simple chart and graph of vehicle speeds.

SPEED (MPH)	NO. OF VEHICLES
BELOW 40	6
40-45	32
45-50	48
50-55	54
55-60	36
ABOVE 60	18

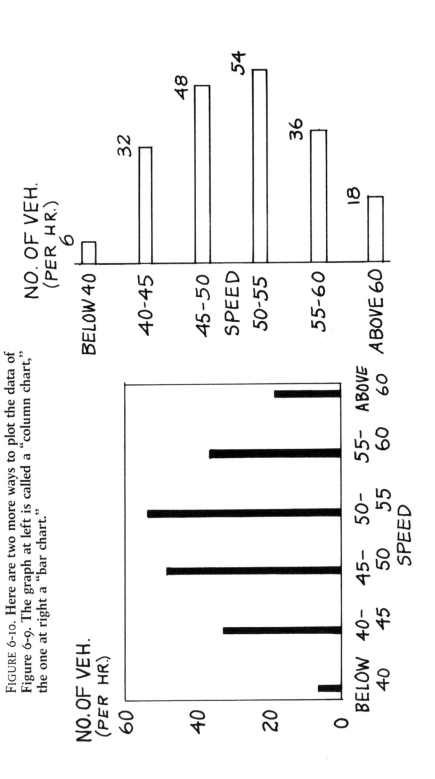

FIGURE 6-10. Here are two more ways to plot the data of Figure 6-9. The graph at left is called a "column chart," the one at right a "bar chart."

Bar Charts Perhaps a better way to graph data in which each data point stands alone and represents a group rather than one point on a curve is to use a *bar graph* or *bar chart*. In such a chart, the length of each bar is made proportional to the number of vehicles in each speed group. The chart shown in the left half of Figure 6-10 can be made by drawing a bar downward from each data point plotted in Figure 6-9. A good idea of the results can be also obtained at a glance from a bar chart. This type of chart can also be made horizontal, as shown in the right half of Figure 6-10. The bars can be made black, white, or colored, as you wish, and for easy reference.

Pie Charts Still another way to graph these data is in a "pie chart." A pie chart is simply a circle that has been divided into segments, like slices of pie. Each piece has been made to a size that represents the size of one of the groups you have measured.

The table in Figure 6-11 shows how the pie is divided up into pieces. The whole pie represents the total number of vehicles, shown on the bottom line as 194. The fraction that each group represents can be calculated as shown in the third column. For example, the group traveling between 40 and 45 miles per hour contained 32 vehicles, which, as a decimal fraction of the whole, is:

$$\frac{32}{194} = 0.16$$

This number can be expressed as the fraction 16/100, or as a percentage, 16%.

In the next column the number of degrees in the slice of pie is calculated: $0.16 \times 360° = 58°$.

In the pie chart at the top of Figure 6-11, you can see that a piece of the pie has been drawn to this size: 58°, or 16% of the whole pie. The other slices have been calculated and drawn (using a protractor) in exactly the same way to divide the whole pie.

FIGURE 6-11. **This is how you could graph the data of Figure 6-9 as a pie chart.**

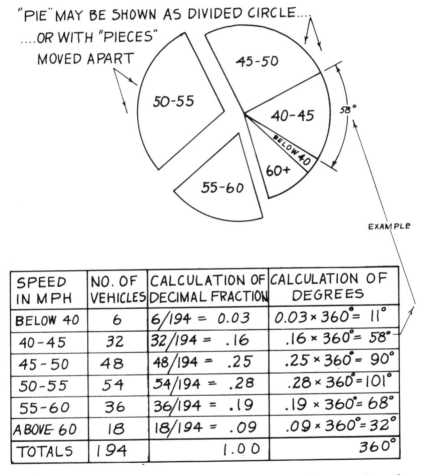

You can see at a glance that the smallest slices of pie are those for "60 +" and "below 40," while the largest slice is that for 50-55 miles per hour. (Note again: the data are imaginary!)

The last kind of chart we will examine has no real scales at all, but uses symbols to show sizes of groups (Figure 6-12). Let's call this a "scatter plot." A compartment is drawn for each speed group, and each vehicle—or, in this case, each five vehicles—for which speed measured is shown by a symbol placed in the proper compartment.

Many types of charts and graphs can be made on a personal computer (word processor) with graphics software. Four such graphs are shown in Figure 6-13.

Now that we have considered five different kinds of graphs for reporting the same data, examine them all again. Which do *you* think shows these particular data in the most understandable way? There is no one kind of graph that is better than all others. The choice will vary from one investigation to another and is often a matter of personal choice. You can use the form that you think suits you and your data best. If one style doesn't seem to work, try another, or design an entirely original one if you prefer.

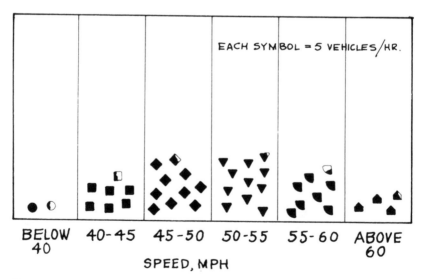

FIGURE 6-12. **This is a way to graph the data of Figure 6-9 as a "scatter plot."**

FIGURE 6-13. The charts shown here were made on a personal computer. Given only the basic data shown, the computer did all the calculations and plotted the graphs and scales shown. Only the caption and scale labels were added. (The data are fictitious).

	A	B
1	NO. OF OCCUPANTS	NO. OF VEHICLES
2	1	36
3	2	44
4	3	21
5	4	11
6	5	8

Basic Data

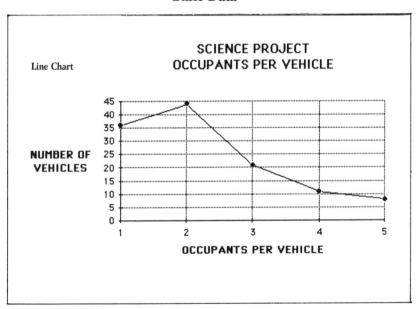

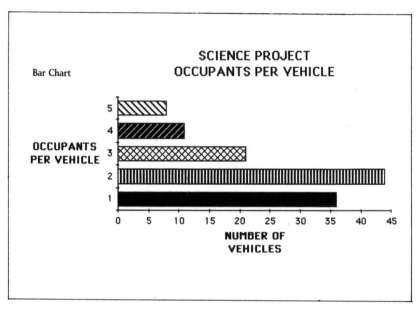

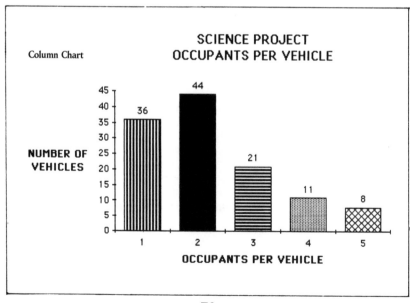

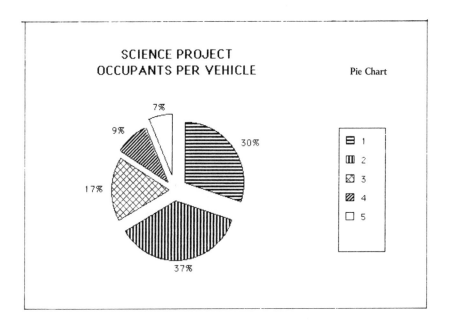

CHOOSING GRAPH SCALES

A word about choosing graph scales is needed here. If, for example, you are measuring temperatures to the nearest whole degree, you should choose a scale that neither exaggerates nor hides the variation you are observing. In Figure 6-14 part (a) shows a vertical scale that is too large. The points appear to be inaccurate because the scale has stretched them too far apart, beyond the need for the 1° accuracy. Part (b) of this figure shows a vertical scale that is too small. The measured change in temperature is poorly shown because the scale has compressed the data points into too small a space. The scale in part (c) of Figure 6-14, on the other hand, is about right for data with an accuracy of 1°. The scale is neither too large nor too small and shows the change in temperature adequately.

TEMP, °C

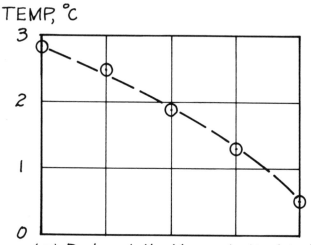

(a.) Data plotted to scale that is too large. Variation is exaggerated.

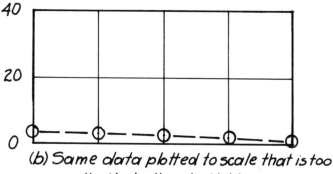

(b) Same data plotted to scale that is too small. Variation is hidden.

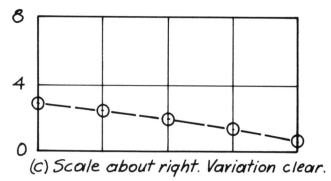

(c) Scale about right. Variation clear.

FIGURE 6-14. Choose a scale that is correct for your data.

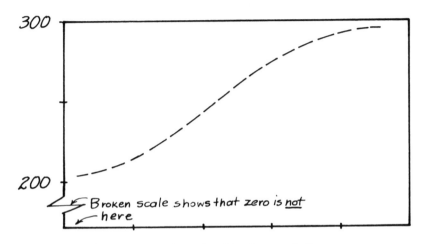

FIGURE 6-15. **This is a graph with a "broken scale."**

It is usually a good idea to start each scale of a graph at "zero," if possible. Doing so will provide a more realistic view of the variation that the graph shows. Figure 6-15 shows why. This graph has a "broken" vertical scale; that is, it does not extend to zero. The curve *seems* to show a change from a very small value at left to a large one at right—an increase that appears to be perhaps three or four times larger than the starting value at left. But that's just an illusion. If we read the scale at left, we see that the graph shows only a variation from a value near 200 to around 300.

Figure 6-16 has a vertical scale that starts at zero. The same data plotted on this graph give a more accurate picture of the variation.

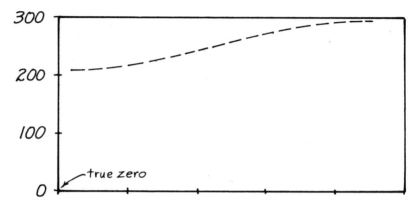

FIGURE 6-16. **The same data from Figure 6-15 are plotted with "true zero" shown.**

The change indicated by the curve is now shown clearly to be only about one-third of the starting value at left—not nearly as large as the upper figure seems to show.

The data can, of course, be plotted to the same scale used in figure 6-15, if desired. such a graph is shown in Figure 6-17. This graph requires much more space than Figure 6-15, which is why broken scales are often used.

A good rule is to avoid broken scales wherever they may give an incorrect impression or picture of the variation. You can examine other broken-scale graphs in this book, including those in the appendix, to test these for yourself.

It is up to you, the investigator, to choose graph scales that will show clearly the variations that you wish to examine, and that you want your readers to grasp quickly and easily. If your first graph does not do the job, don't hesitate to try again with another choice of scales or another kind of graph.

If you have access to a computer with a graphics program, and are skilled in using such a program, you may be able to make your plots

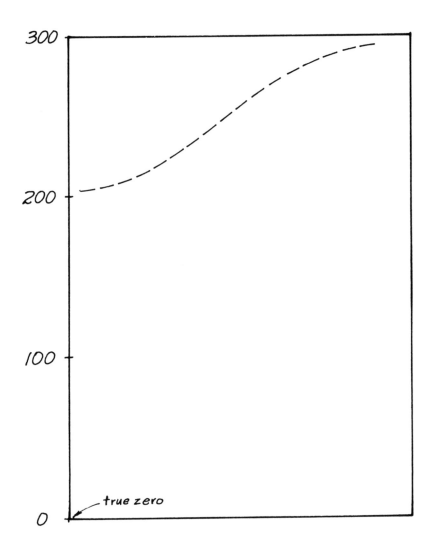

FIGURE 6-17. **Here is another way of plotting the data in Figure 6-15.**

and graphs by machine. But in any case, you must be able to design your graphs to fit your particular needs. You may find hand-plotting faster and more suitable for your needs. Several samples of computer-generated graphs are shown in Figure 6-15.

GRAPHS IN THE MEDIA

Graphs and charts are used for many purposes besides scientific investigations. They are used in newspapers, news magazines, lecture slides, and informational articles of all kinds in which the author wants to give a quick picture of what he or she is writing or talking about. You can learn more about graphs by examining the ones you see in publications. Some samples are shown in the appendix. You might want to practice reading graphs like these, analyzing what they show, and looking for new ideas that you might use in reporting your own project.

Remember that good graphing will not only help you to analyze and understand your experimental results, but should also help you to present and explain your results to your readers in a clear and interesting way.

CHAPTER 7

DRAWING YOUR CONCLUSIONS

I once reviewed a science-fair display by a team that had done a fine job on an investigative project. Their display showed what they did, how they did it, samples of their equipment, and graphs of their data. But something was obviously missing. In their hurry to

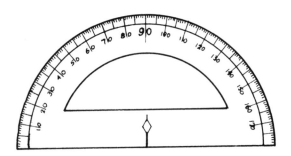

complete their project, they had forgotten what their viewers would be most interested in: the *results*. They had forgotten to draw and present their *conclusions*.

A scientific report without conclusions is like a joke without a punch line, or a ball game without a final score, or a mystery without a solution. Without conclusions, the whole point of your investigation is missing. the conclusions from your project are its most valuable product—indeed, its whole purpose.

Many students give so much attention to the display and to the competitive aspects of their project that they do a hurried job toward the end of their investigation and slight or forget the task of drawing and reporting specific, concise conclusions. No matter how eye-catching your display, nothing will make up for weak or missing conclusions. You have told your reader in the first part of your report what you hoped to accomplish. He or she will be looking for the results you promised.

The conclusions you can draw are probably right in the graphs of your data. Set them down in clear, simple sentences, one thought per sentence:

1. The percentage of all vehicles exceeding the 55 mph speed limit was_____.
2. The percentage is larger (smaller) for heavy trucks than for automobiles,_____compared to_____.
3. The greatest speed measured was_____.
4. More than_____% to exceeded the speed limit by more than 10 mph.
5. The results show that vehicles on this highway are (are not) observing the speed limit to an adequate degree.

If you find that you can't write conclusions for your investigation in short, clear sentences, you probably have not yet completed your analysis. Go back to the data and spend some more time with it. What were you looking for? What did your investigation show? Ask questions that can be answered with simple one-topic, one-line conclusions:

▲ Did liquids take different amounts of time to cool down (or warm up) in different containers?

▲ Which one was best?

▲ Which one was worst?

▲ Why?

▲ What do your results mean to you and/or to your reader?

▲ What other things of importance did you discover?

Don't hesitate to present all the important conclusions that your results entitle you to make. You have not only the right to do this, but also the obligation.

On the other hand, you should be careful not to claim more than your data justify. If you claim more than you have really discovered

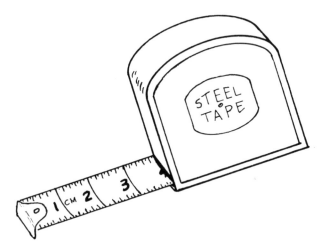

about your topic, your reader (or the judge) will not be impressed. Remember, he's looking at your data, too, and interpreting it for himself. If you claim something not borne out by your data, you will be found out. It pays to be totally honest, and it doesn't hurt to show a little caution and a bit of modesty, too.

If you have doubts about any of your findings, state them. If you now see some other interesting, useful things that should be done in a future investigation, describe them. Personally, I like to see a researcher look ahead and point out very briefly in his or her conclusions questions and topics that still remain to be investigated. Any scientist knows that all investigations are limited and that more work could—and perhaps will—follow yours. It adds to your stature as an investigator to show that you know what came before your investigation and what is likely to come after it, and that you have an honest, realistic view of what you have accomplished.

CHAPTER 8

REPORTING YOUR RESULTS

No one can tell you exactly how to report the results of your project. There is no single, best way to report a scientific investigation. Each project has its own requirements, each scientist has his or her own style, and each audience has different interests

and needs. As the investigator, you can report your results in any way you think most appropriate.

But it is important to your readers that your results be presented in a logical manner and give them the answers they need as quicky and painlessly as possible.

It doesn't matter whether your report is a written paper, an oral presentation, or a display using charts and posters. Your audience will expect you to tell them in an orderly way why you performed your investigation, what you did, how you did it, what results you obtained, and what conclusions you have drawn.

THE WRITTEN REPORT

Let's look first at the ingredients of a written report. An oral report or a science-fair display, which will be covered later, can be made by using parts of the written report.

The basic parts that a written report should contain are generally the following:

SUMMARY
INTRODUCTION
METHODS & EQUIPMENT
RESULTS
DISCUSSION (OR RESULTS & DISCUSSION)
CONCLUSIONS (OR CONCLUDING REMARKS)
REFERENCES (OR BIBLIOGRAPHY)
FIGURES (These can be distributed through the text or grouped at the end of the report.)

Surprisingly enough, although reports are printed in this general order, they are seldom either *written* or *read* in this order! Most people who are looking for information on a particular topic won't start at the beginning of a report but will read the Conclusions and Summary first to find out quickly what was done and whether the results of the investigation might be of interest or of use to them. If the reader finds the work interesting, he or she may then read the rest of the report in any order; for example, perhaps the Figures next, then the Results & Discussion, with the Introduction and Methods sections last.

The researcher/scientist might write the section on Methods & Equipment first, then Results & Discussion. Then these sections can be used to write the Conclusions. Introduction and Summary sections are likely to be written last, even though they appear at the beginning of the finished report.

Here are some suggestions as to what should be put into each of these sections:

INTRODUCTION. In this section the investigator introduces the project to the audience. The author may bring the reader up to date as to the status of the problem he or she has chosen to investigate, or as to what work has been done on it previously. The problem that was investigated can then be described, and the way in which it was investigated can be outlined very briefly.

METHODS & EQUIPMENT. This section describes the methods and equipment used in the investigation. Enough detail should be included so that another researcher could repeat your tests if he or she wished, or could check your results by doing the investigation in a different way, if that seemed appropriate. (In general, science does not accept a new discovery until it has been confirmed by at least one more investigator.) Photographs or diagrams of equipment are very desirable as illustrations in this section.

RESULTS & DISCUSSION. In this section (or in two separate sections) the investigator sets forth the results that have been obtained. These can be in tables or in graphs, as described earlier in Chapter 6. They should present not only the basic data but also the comparisons and analysis that show what the results mean. These figures should be described and discussed in enough detail to give the reader the information needed to follow your analysis and understand your conclusions.

This section may be broken down by using subheadings for individual topics as required. For example:

▲ Measurements of automobile speeds
▲ Measurements of truck speeds
▲ Measurements at different times of day
▲ Averages of vehicle speeds

Subheadings may be used in any area of your report where they will help you to organize the report better or help your reader to follow it or find what he or she is looking for more easily.

CONCLUSIONS. If the previous section has been properly done, the conclusions drawn may be taken (often lifted word for word) from the discussion and listed here. If no sharply defined individual conclusions are possible, more general statements may be written in a section titled Concluding Remarks.

SUMMARY. If you have completed the sections described above, you now have the material with which to prepare the shortest section in your report, the Summary. In a few sentences you should describe what you did and the conclusions you have drawn. Leave out the details. If the reader is interested after reading your Summary, he or she can find the details in the other sections. Your task here is to give the reader a quick sketch of the entire report in a short paragraph or two. If you have done your work well in the other sections,the material you need here can be lifted from these sections, again, sometimes word for word.

You will, of course, want to place at the front of your report a neat title page that gives such information as the title of your project, the author, and the place and date. If your report is a long one, you may want to place a table of contents after the title page. You should list your chapters by title and page.

Good report writing is not always easy, but the job will be easier if your investigation has been well done, and if you have put a great deal of thought into it.

It goes almost without saying that correct grammar, punctuation, and spelling must be used throughout. Incorrect English is no more acceptable than incorrect arithmetic. Don't expect to produce a good report in one draft. Let your rough draft "cool" for a couple of days, then go over it critically. Rework or rewrite the areas that need attention.

A typed report has many advantages—it can be neater, more attractive, and more easily read. A word processor is especially valuable for such work because it will give you the ability to rearrange and alter your text so easily. If you do not have access to a typewriter or a word processor, prepare your report carefully in your most legible handwriting.

Photographs of your equipment, specimens, results, or of any phase of your investigation will be an asset to your report. If you do not have adequate camera equiment, see if you can find a friend or an amateur photographer who does. Many of them would be glad to have a chance to keep his or her skills sharp by helping you with photographs for your project. You should supply the film and other materials. Your photographer may even develop and print your pictures for you or you can have them done by a development service. Have prints made large enough to show what you want them to show.

Place the photographs in your report wherever they are needed. Be sure that they are clear, sharp, and correctly exposed. Poor photographs do not help a good report.

If diagrams of equipment or test setups are needed, make sketches first in pencil. Then draw them carefully with ink or felt-tip pens. Use rulers and drafting curves if you can to produce as neat a job as possible. Some suggestions for lettering any figures are shown in Figure 8-1. If you have access to a word processor, you may have a choice of many lettering styles and sizes that may enhance the looks of your report and its figures. But neat, skillful, hand lettering may be faster and more flexible.

Keep your writing simple. The following suggestions should be remembered:

- ▲ Keep sentences short.
- ▲ Prefer the simple to the complex.
- ▲ Use the familiar word; avoid unnecessary words.
- ▲ Tie in with reader's experiences, and use terms which the reader can readily understand and picture.
- ▲ Write the way you talk. To test your writing, read it aloud. If it is difficult to read, or sounds dreary or wordy, rewrite it.
- ▲ Make full use of variety, but choose the precise technical word even if repetition is necessary.
- ▲ Above all, write to express, not to impress.

Remember that you are *the* authority on your project. You know more about it than anyone else in the world. Your task in reporting it to your readers, listeners, or judges is to convey information to them as simply, concisely, and rapidly as possible. Take them by the hand and lead them through what you want them to know.

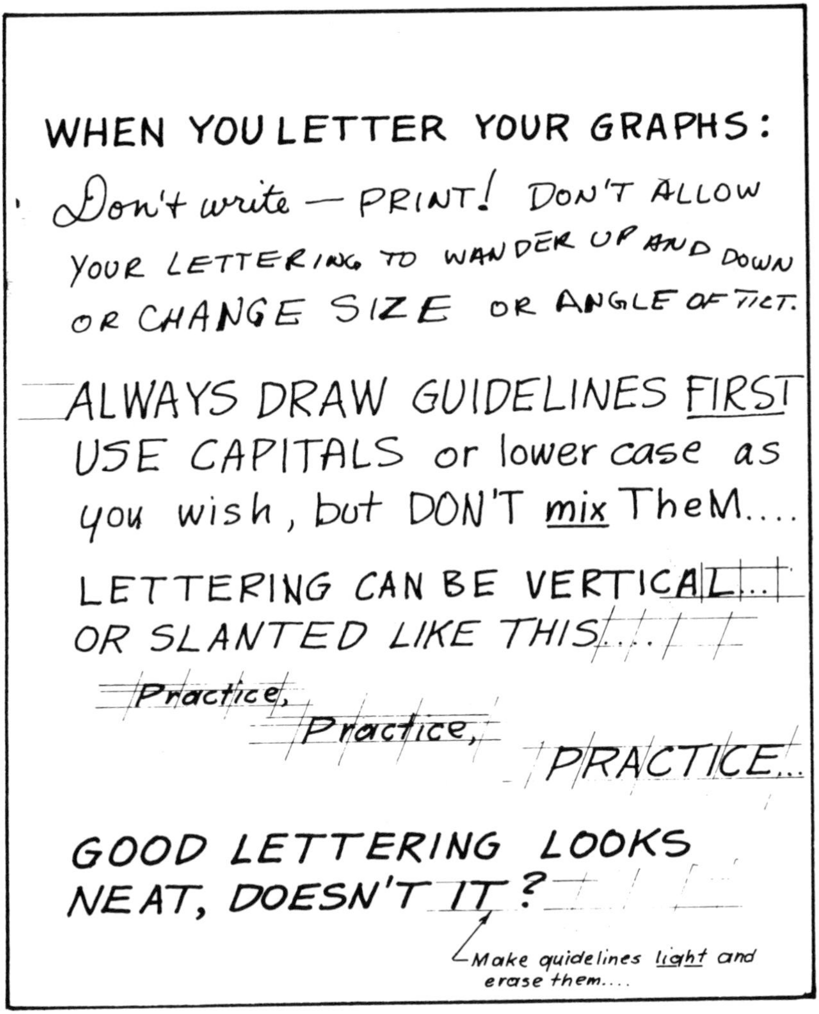

WHEN YOU LETTER YOUR GRAPHS:

Don't write — PRINT! DON'T ALLOW YOUR LETTERING TO WANDER UP AND DOWN OR CHANGE SIZE OR ANGLE OF TILT.

ALWAYS DRAW GUIDELINES FIRST USE CAPITALS or lower case as you wish, but DON'T mix TheM....

LETTERING CAN BE VERTICAL... OR SLANTED LIKE THIS....

Practice, Practice, PRACTICE...

GOOD LETTERING LOOKS NEAT, DOESN'T IT?

Make guidelines light and erase them....

FIGURE 8-I. **Lettering on your graph should be done neatly and clearly.**

THE SCIENCE-FAIR DISPLAY (REPORT)

Science-fair projects are usually reported in some sort of poster or table display, at which the student is expected to explain his or her work. The form of reporting has the advantage that students can display their experiments or test equipment and use showmanship to good advantage. But it also provides a disadvantage if the student is unable to discuss his or her work with the judges and respond to questions. The best preparation for any science-fair report is a project that is carefully performed according to the methods and procedures described earlier in this book.

A science-fair display prepared by the student can be anything from a copy of his or her report to simple posters. Or it may be a high-powered spread of fancy posters, equipment, and graphs of test results. The choice will depend upon the rules or traditions of the fair and upon the abilities and desires of the student.

Whatever the kind of display (or report) chosen, it should do exactly the same overall job as the reporting process described earlier in this chapter. It should answer the following questions.

▲ Why did you choose this topic?
▲ What did you do?
▲ How did you do it?
▲ What are your results and conclusions?

Your display should be concise and eye catching. It should cover only the highlights of your project. You need not attempt to cover all the details of your project or all of your conclusions. Give your viewers a quick picture of your project and a few of the more exciting or relevant conclusions. Think about what you might like to see and hear if you were in *their* shoes. Plan your display accordingly.

The design and construction of science-fair displays are beyond the scope of this book. But the basic tools are simple and easy to obtain. Posterboard and felt markers are readily available in a variety of colors. With a little careful planning, practice (see Figure 8-1), and some patience, very attrative charts and posters can be made that will do the job of communicating with your audience.

Remember that the quality of your display is important, but the real test of your project lies in the quality of the job you have done in planning and performing the investigation and in analyzing the results.

APPENDIX
(SAMPLES OF CHARTS AND GRAPHS)

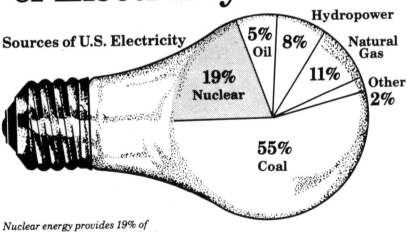

Nuclear Energy is America's #2 Source of Electricity

Sources of U.S. Electricity

Hydropower

5% Oil

8%

Natural Gas

19% Nuclear

11%

Other 2%

55% Coal

Nuclear energy provides 19% of U.S. electricity, and the contribution of nuclear is growing.

Source: Edison Electric Institute, 1988

For more information, contact: **U.S. Council for Energy Awareness,** 1776 I Street, N.W., Washington, D.C. 20006

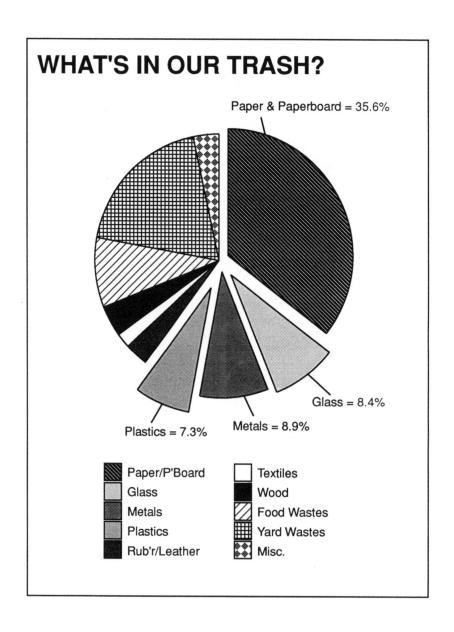

PLASTIC PRODUCTS RECYCLED IN 1988

150
million
lbs.

70
million
lbs.

Milk, Water,
Juice, Detergent, etc.
Container
Recycling

Soft-Drink
Bottle
Recycling

More than 220 million pounds of plastic containers were recycled during 1988.

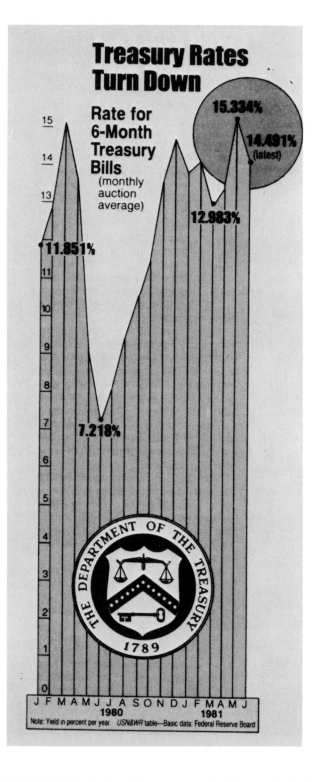

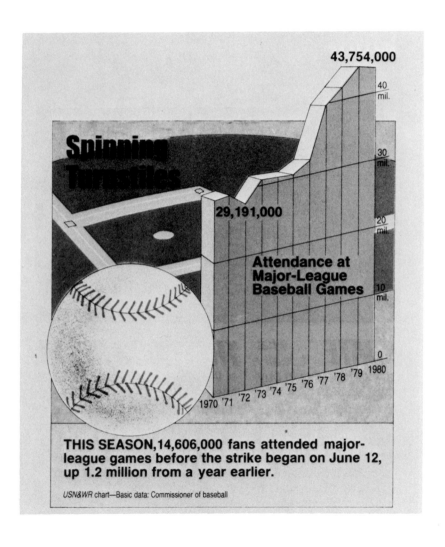

Spinning Turnstiles

43,754,000

29,191,000

Attendance at Major-League Baseball Games

40 mil.

30 mil.

20 mil.

10 mil.

0

1970 '71 '72 '73 '74 '75 '76 '77 '78 '79 1980

THIS SEASON,14,606,000 fans attended major-league games before the strike began on June 12, up 1.2 million from a year earlier.

USN&WR chart—Basic data: Commissioner of baseball

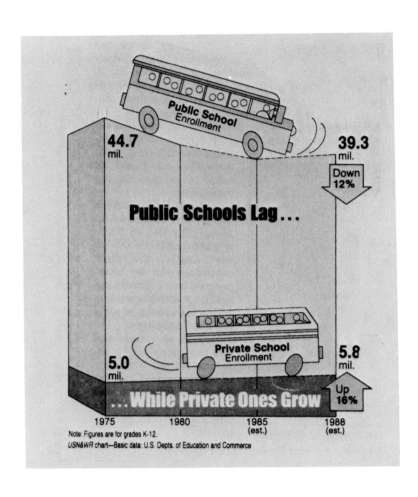

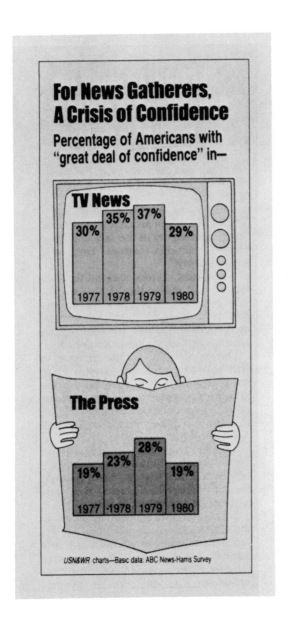

BIBLIOGRAPHY

A number of books have been published on science experiments and projects for a variety of purposes. This bibliography will attempt only to categorize and sample the types of books available.

There are relatively few books that deal directly with investigative projects. Three very useful books that treat various aspects of such projects are:

Moorman, Tom. *How to Make Your Science Project More Scientific.* Atheneum, 1974.

Stepp, Ann. *Setting Up a Science Project.* Prentice Hall, 1965.

Vandeman and McDonald. *Nuts and Bolts; A Matter-of-Fact Guide to Science-Fair Projects.* The Science Man Press.

Four other books of more limited application are:

Source Book for Science Teaching.
UNESCO. (Some information on science equipment, resources, experiments).

Barr, George. *Research Ideas for For Young Scientists.* McGraw Hill, 1958. (A good introduction to very simple measurements and investigations.)

Diamond, Solomon. *The World of Probability.* Basic Books, Inc., 1964. (A beginner's book on statistics—but still quite technical.)

Gardner, Robert. *Energy Projects for Young Scientists.* Franklin Watts, 1987.

Goodwin, Peter H. *Engineering Projects for Young Scientists.* Franklin Watts, 1987

James, Elizabeth and Carole Barkin. *What Do You Mean by "Average"?* Lothrop, Lee & Shepard, 1978.

Most books on science-fair projects deal mainly with exotic, higher-level (high school) projects rather than with investigative, beginner-level projects. Two typical titles:

Ideas for Science Fair Projects. Arco Publishing Co., 1962.

Sawyer, R. W. and R. A. Farmer *New Ideas for Science Fair Projects.* Arco Publishing Co., 1967

A large number of books have been published on "science experiments" and are widely available in school libraries. Most of these books present a number of simple science activities, experiments, demonstrations, and even science "tricks." The point of each is usually to illustrate a single science principle or phenomenon. The science student may find such books interesting, and perhaps a source of ideas. It sould be noted, however, that most of these "experiments" are *not* investigative in nature, nor are they adequate to constitute a true "science project."

INDEX

ABOUT THE AUTHOR

Norman F. Smith was an aeronautical research scientist with NACA (the predecessor of NASA) for fifteen years and in that capacity performed and reported numerous research investigations. He later held a variety of engineering and executive postions with NASA during the Mercury, Gemini, and Apollo projects. He served as technical editor for many research reports and post-launch reports for NACA/NASA, and for a major book on space technology.

Mr. Smith took early retirement near the end of the Apollo Program to work full time as a science consultant, author, and lecturer. He is the author of numerous articles, filmstrips, movies, and fourteen books on a variety of science subjects.